Leylines

Katherine Buchanan

Leylines

Acknowledgements

Some of these poems have been previously published.
An earlier version of 'Golden Silence' was published in
Funne Stuffe 2000 (Issue 51) under the title 'Whoever Said',
'Nightmares' was first published in *Funne Stuffe 2000* (Issue 51),
and 'The Craft' in *The Dawn 2000* (October).

Leylines
ISBN 978 1 76041 728 4
Copyright © text Katherine Buchanan 2019
Cover image: Katherine Buchanan

First published 2019 by
Ginninderra Press
PO Box 3461 Port Adelaide 5015 Australia
www.ginninderrapress.com.au

Contents

Leylines	7
Darkness and Light	8
Nomura	9
Coexistence	10
The Promise	11
Spiral Dance	12
Haiku for the Seasons	13
Bay of Plenty	14
Black on White	15
Inheritance	16
Dust and Sunset	17
Imagination	18
A Sorrow	19
Our World	20
Meditation I	21
Golden Silence	22
Gunns and Eucalypts	23
Stages	24
When	25
Ideas	26
Untitled	27
The Long Goodbye	28
Songs From the Goddess	29
Beneath the Moon	30
Mother, Sister, Spirit	31
Artemis	32
Whispers of Reincarnation and Magic	33
The Wheel of Life	34
Meditation II	35
Nightmares	36

The Craft	38
A Single Tear	39
Seasons	40
Solstice	41
Sunrise	42
Unattainable	43
Haiku on Peace	44

Leylines

Leylines guide the spirit
(*traveller   merchant   worshipper*)
Invisible etchings, hidden below
the narrow, well worn paths that
criss-cross the earth
Linking sacred places –
standing stones, henges and springs
Waiting for the next pilgrim
to wander the leylines

Darkness and Light

Darkness and light
flicker alternately.
Denied reflections
of mortality.
Don't look inside –
Too hard. Too real.
It's easier to point out
that darkness in others.

Nomura

Nomura – monster jellyfish
polyps gather off the Chinese coast
in billions.

A once-in-40-year bloom
that drifts on the current to Japan
eating and growing all the way.

200 kilos and 2 metres across –
each one a sumo wrestler
filling trawler nets, jelly oozing,
tonnes of waste.

Scientists blame
rising sea temperatures,
water pollution, eutrophication,
over-fishing.

Local fishermen admit there are no predators left –
they've ended up in fish market stalls.
And now there is an exponential growth of monsters.

Japanese fleets are hauled up –
dry docked.
Empty nets stored on racks to wait it out
the once-in-40-year bloom.

Same as last year.

Coexistence

Can human frailty
and nuclear weapons
coexist?

Oceans of skin and flesh and tarmac
Provide the illusion of peace

The Promise

An icy wind blows in from the south
Steely grey clouds hang low in the sky
Ominous
Slow moving
Filled with the promise of snow

Spiral Dance

ghostly mist

    a swirling

        spiral dance

            eyes close, lips part

        gently caress

    flakes melt

satisfy my thirst

Haiku for the Seasons

I

dry heat of summer
scorch the golden desert sand
harsh, unrelenting

II

russet autumn leaf
send ever growing ripples
silently outward

III

snow-capped winter peaks
sunlit reflections, tranquil
on still, deep waters

IV

spring proclaims new life
fragrant jasmine, blossoming
touches hearts deeply

Bay of Plenty

47,000 tonnes of *Liberian Rena*
stranded on a reef, back broken.
Rusted shell cracked through
Spilling its black yolk into the bay.

Helicopters fly low
spraying dispersant.
The futile effort
only adds to the pollution

Stinking globs of tarry oil litter the beach.
Dead fish and birds wash up on shore
among the flotsam of deer skins and
half-cooked burger patties.

Volunteers rescue survivors
penguins and gulls.
Glossy eyes blinking slowly
camouflaged in matted feathers.

Locals shovel muck off the sand.
Toxic residue stains fingers black
dissolving the numbers
off a mobile phone.

Black on White

Simple thoughts and
silent wonderings
drift from pen to paper

Whispered words, framed
black with white
each a separate moment

One to another, flowing
over the line
to become reality

Making sense
of nothing
to no one

Inheritance

Desire – needful and selfish.
Indulgent worshippers
satisfy their avarice.

Desperate – a few cry out.
Thin distant wails
echo the warning.

All that's left?
An empty inheritance
marking the death of humanity.

Dust and Sunset

Dust and sunset
Images and memories
Captured on an everlasting canvas
Painted across the mind

Old growth forests, oceans and shores
Hues of green, turquoise and gold
Photographic negatives
Developed behind closed lids

Imagination

Alone in the dark
sounds infiltrate reality
Imagination takes over
and runs rampant

The thunder of rain on a cold, tin roof
becomes a beast
Red-eyed and clawed
scrambling over the corrugations

The low branch scraping against the window
is the shadow of a man
His long yellow nails
dragged screeching down the glass

Howling winds ripping through the trees
are wild beasts raging closer and closer, until
whipping around the house
they are gone

That groaning, screaming agony
not ancient pines uprooted in the storm
but the violence of an unseen battle
pitched close by

Alone and vulnerable in the night
Even though you know what is real
and what is imagined…

Can you be sure?

A Sorrow

Gaia cries
and her children ignore her sorrow.
Listen to her weep.
Taste her tears.
Feel her pain.

Our World

This world was left
for us to watch
while it was in our care

What will we do
when we are asked
about its poor repair

Will we explain away
this mess
and why it looks this way

What will we say
in our defence
should we expect to pay

We are like children
this world our toy
its outcome blamed on fate

Now we've decided
to change our ways
I wonder if it's too late

The children try
to right our wrongs
out of our filth they climb

We're slowly dying
one by one
I hope we still have time

Meditation I

The corner of my mind – a haven

silent – sacred

only the pulse

to focus on

Golden Silence

Have you ever

paused under a rainforest canopy
to hear the echo of a bower bird call?

or rested on the sand
to hear the waves meet the shore?

sailed on the sea
to hear the snap of the sails in the wind?

or washed in the mist of a waterfall
to hear the thunderous roar of the cascade?

Nature is never silent

Just listen

Gunns and Eucalypts

Tasmania's compensation shame
A 35-million-dollar payout,
twice the amount required
to settle the government's debt dispute –
23 million for Gunns to relinquish its rights over
Tasmania's native forests,
but not to stop the pulp mill.
11.5 million to pay out Gunns' debt to Forestry Tasmania

Leaked emails and memos
imply a seedier side to the deal
reveal the order to remove a table of
dioxin concentrations around George Town.
Claims that disclosure that could bring down
two governments and the company –
poor things

Tasmania's ancient rainforests
barely protected, under threat
from a legally invalid pulp mill.
Gunns argues the reality of a forest industry
that chipping for profit
is better than burning waste wood –
carbon credits up in smoke

Triazine herbicides – atrazin, simazine
chemicals banned in Europe
still used in our delicate water catchments.
Contaminated drinking water for Orford, St Marys, Macquarie
poisoned Rubicon and Little Swanport Rivers –
alarmist or cautious

Stages

Whispers, as the lights go down.
Silence,
inhaled with a sweep of blood-red velvet.
And so it begins.

Paint and glitz and larger-than
lives performed for rows of faceless
formless shadows,
barely seen.

The vast homogenous voyeur
carried along
with each inflexion and emotion,
leaves the day-to-day for a while.

Lost in light and movement, love and hate
played upon a stage.
Until the velvet exhales.
The journey begun with silence – ends with a roar.

When

Remember when hot chips from the takeaway on the corner
were wrapped in newspaper,
came with malt vinegar and cost 20 cents?

Remember when a brown paper bag
packed full of lollies,
cost 5 cents and lasted all day?

Remember when the proceeds of a Saturday afternoon
spent collecting and crushing aluminium cans
made you rich?

Ideas

The mind wanders
drifting on waves of thought
that come and go
lifted from the crest of one idea
to the next

Untitled

Finding time that allows for thought
is a precious commodity.

Aim to steal both –
that is, time and thought.

The Long Goodbye

When one of two becomes
the soul keeper
of memories shared no longer

When one grows up, while one grows down
intimacy fading
a life together stolen

A shrinking, eggshell-covered world
of swings and roundabouts
snakes and ladders

Mental potholes and minefields

But music makes me happy
and ocean song soothes for a while
embrace the moments of calm while you can

Nancy said it best

The longest goodbye

Songs From the Goddess

Listen to her voice in your heart
Hear her whisper
Feel the songs from the Goddess
Speak from within

Beneath the Moon

Beneath the Moon
In silver light
You kneel to pray
To Her tonight

Light the candle
Watch the flame
Raise the Power
Call Her name

Sense Her presence
Feel Her kiss
See Her Spirit
In the mist

Hear Her whisper
Close your eyes
Know that you
Are with the wise

Honour Mother, Maiden, Crone
Trust that you are not alone
Keep Her Blessings in your heart
Merry Meet and Merry Part

Mother, Sister, Spirit

Earth Mother
Show me your secrets
Share your wisdom with me
So that I might know
Let me understand
What you are teaching me
What you are asking of me

Moon Sister
Show me your secrets
Share your wisdom with me
So that I might know
Let me understand
What you are teaching me
What you are asking of me

Ancient Spirit
Show me your secrets
Share your wisdom with me
So that I might know
Let me understand
What you are teaching
What you are asking of me

I am listening

Mother
I feel your presence in the tender breeze
Caressing autumn leaves
Showing
Sharing
Teaching
Asking

Sister
I see your power in the ebb and flow
Of the ocean's tides
Showing
Sharing
Teaching
Asking

Spirit
I hear your whisper in my heart and soul
Within my very core
Showing
Sharing
Teaching
Asking

And I hear

Artemis

Goddess of the Sacred Moon,
Chaste, and ever pure.
Virgin huntress, bow held high,
You run with the beasts.
Warrior Goddess, fierce and brave,
Victory is yours.
Goddess of the Sacred Moon,
Artemis

Whispers of Reincarnation and Magic

Shall I speak of the mysteries?
While you listen
To stories of life, death and rebirth

Shall I tell of the magic?
The magic of living
Magic both seen and unseen

Shall I share with you
Mysteries of things unknown?
Are you willing to hear?

Come
Follow me
Hear the whispers

The Wheel of Life

The Wheel of Life spins round and round
Sometimes we're up; sometimes we're down
But deep inside what keeps us sane
Is knowing life spins round again

   Cycles ebb and cycles flow
   The Wheel of Life, the journey home
   Seasons change and seasons pass
   From birth to death, each has their path

      Life is full, we live to learn
      From dawn to dawn, we journey on
      A chance to love, a chance to grow
      From Mother Earth, the chance to know

         Each time we live, each time we die
         Our souls return to Earth to try
         To live in Light and share our love
         While watched upon by Gods above

            The Wheel of Life spins 'round and 'round
            Sometimes we're up; sometimes we're down
            Though a human shell may fade
            We know our souls live on again

Meditation II

This Sacred Space…this haven.

A world of my own creation.

Hidden…in a corner of my mind.

Silence…overpowering.

Time…standing still.

Only the motion of life,

the blood pulsing through my body,

to focus on.

Nightmares

In dark of night
The terrors come
Put dreams to flight
The death knoll drum

Chills and panic
Fears and dread
Don't scream aloud
You'll wake the dead

A beating heart
Pounds in your ears
Pray that darkness
Hides your fears

Deep within
Your fear has grown
Voices whisper
Unseen, unknown

Will you wake
Or will you sleep
Will your soul
The darkness keep

Fingers grasping
Hold you fast
Will this nightmare
Be your last

Then break of dawn
The rays of light
Shadows vanish
Fears take flight

Tear stained pillow
Trembling heart
A prayer of thanks
Nightmares depart

The Craft

As is above
So is below
Open the Circle
Feel the energy grow

Raising the Power
The spell has begun
Do what ye will
And harm ye none

Remember the Law of Return
Times three
Walk in the Light
And Blessed Be

A Single Tear

Empty words
Falling on deaf ears
Making no difference
In a bitter world

Selfish needs
Destroying concern for fellow man
Turning friends
Into untrusted enemies

A single tear
Shed for what is lost
Coursing down the bare cheek
Of the planet's surface

A single tear
For the death of humanity

A single tear
For what cannot be undone

A single tear
And that is all

Seasons

The natural cycle continues
And we silently watch the seasons

Summer, Autumn, Winter and Spring
Mark the passing of endless eons

Solstice

Sunlight on the East horizon
Gently greets the Solstice dawn
Rays of gold reflect on water
Rising Sun on Solstice morn

Honouring the Summer Solstice
Feel the warmth of longest day
Queen of Summer, Mother Goddess
Celebrate in a special way

Golden Sun drifts overhead
Gives Summer heat in Summer sky
Feel His rays shine down upon you
Bathing Mother Earth from high

Sunlight on the West horizon
Bids farewell to Mother Earth
Paints the clouds this rosy evening
Setting until His rebirth

Sunrise

Sweetly calls the nightingale
From branches high above
Softly sings the mudlark
While quietly coos the dove

Gently cry the creatures
As the day begins to dawn
And golden rays of sunlight

Creep slowly 'cross the lawn
Now the sun has risen
And nightly shadows fled
Warmth has gathered round us
To raise us from our bed

Each day begins with sounds of life
The songs of peace and love
Perhaps we all could start our day
Seeing beauty from above

Unattainable

Absence of war
Presence of harmony and friendship
Freedom from strife

Haiku on Peace

The state of silence
Stillness and serenity
Calm tranquillity

www.ingramcontent.com/pod-product-compliance
Lightning Source LLC
Chambersburg PA
CBHW062206100526
44589CB00014B/1979